revelations

Unraveling Biblical Mysteries

LARRY MASSA

ISBN 978-1-68517-845-1 (paperback)
ISBN 978-1-68517-846-8 (digital)

Christian Faith Publishing
832 Park Avenue
Meadville, PA 16335
www.christianfaithpublishing.com

Printed in the United States of America

CONTENTS

ACKNOWLEDGMENTS

I want to thank the Holy Spirit for giving me the spiritual gifts of prophecy and discernment; specifically, the ability to use inductive logic to understand God's word. I try to use those gifts to glorify Him.

I also acknowledge, through blog comments on my website crazyaboutgod.com and through dealing with a number of Christian organizations, that many people have become biblically illiterate. This book is an attempt to help those and others better understand the Bible.

INTRODUCTION

Inductive Logic

Inductive reasoning is an approach to logical thinking that involves making generalizations based on specific details. It begins with identifying facts known to be true or false and collecting observations that are specific but limited in scope. Then, a generalized conclusion is formulated which explains all the facts and observations. It is the explanation that is most likely true in light of the accumulated evidence but may not be exactly correct.

With deductive reasoning, one starts with a generalization or theory and then tests it by applying it to specific incidents. Deductive reasoning is using general ideas to reach a specific conclusion.

Here is a simplified example to understand the difference between deductive and inductive reasoning.

Suppose there is a road with an *S* curve near your house. The speed limit is fifteen miles per hour. As you drive toward it, you know that if you drive much faster than the limit, you will wreck your car. That is deductive logic.

However, say you come upon a car wreck at that curve. Law enforcement are there to determine how the wreck happened. They are collecting as many facts as possible. There are skid marks being measured. Weather conditions are noted. The car type, age, and condition are collected. Witness accounts are being taken. All other facts available are being compiled. You know one of the officers and ask him what happened. He replies, based upon all the information present, the victim attempted to drive around the curve at forty miles per hour, lost control, and wrecked the car. That is inductive reasoning.

Here is where using inductive reasoning to solve a biblical puzzle and using it to recreate a traffic accident differs. One can use physics to animate the accident on a computer to *observe* what probably happened.

Developing a most probable explanation of complicated biblical concepts cannot be tested beyond assuring the explanation does not refute anything else in the Bible (the Bible never contradicts itself).

Therefore, one cannot be dogmatic about the interpretation. It remains simply the one most probable. This book uses inductive logic to arrive at clear and *most probable* explanations of difficult-to-understand passages (mysteries).

MYSTERY 1

Jesus

Jesus is the best-known name in the world and has been for two thousand years. It polarizes mankind. Some people and religions hate hearing about Him. Others are drawn to Him, revere Him, and even worship Him. But the fact is, most of both groups do not really know who He is.

To understand who Jesus is, one must start with a couple of biblical facts. First, there is only one God. It is explicit that He is a singular *One*. The Bible provides multiple references to this but only one example is sufficient.

"'The most important one,' answered Jesus, 'is this: 'Hear, O Israel: The Lord our God, the Lord is one'" (Mark 12:29 NIV).

However, a strange thing is stated in the book of Genesis.

"God said, Let Us [Father, Son, and Holy Spirit] make mankind in Our image, after Our likeness, and let them have complete authority over the fish of the sea, the birds of the air, the [tame] beasts, and over all of the earth, and over everything that creeps upon the earth" (Genesis 1:26).

The second fact is revealed in this verse. God refers to Himself as *Us*. When the Bible states God is *One* (singular) but refers to Himself as *Us* (plural), we encounter an antinomy. An antinomy is a paradox. An example is "The only thing that doesn't change is that everything changes." When the paradox involves philosophy or religion, the word is fine-tuned to *antinomy*.

One is encountered when two reasonable conclusions cannot be true at the same time. *God is one,* yet *God is three,* is impossible to conceive as being simultaneously true to our finite minds.

Jesus tells us that although God is One (singular), He manifests Himself as three entities; He is one, and everyone sees that *One* in Jesus:

> *If you had known Me [had learned to recognize Me], you would also have known My Father. From now on, you know Him and have seen Him.*
>
> *Philip said to Him, Lord, show us the Father [cause us to see the Father—that is all we ask]; then we shall be satisfied.*
>
> *Jesus replied, Have I been with all of you for so long a time, and do you not recognize and know Me yet, Philip? Anyone who has seen Me has seen the Father. How can you say then, Show us the Father?*
>
> *Do you not believe that I am in the Father, and that the Father is in Me? What I am telling you I do not say on My own authority and of My own accord; but the Father Who lives continually in Me does the (His) works (His own miracles, deeds of power).*
>
> *Believe Me that I am in the Father and the Father in Me; or else believe Me for the sake of the [very] works themselves. [If you cannot trust Me, at least let these works that I do in My Father's name convince you.]*
>
> *I assure you, most solemnly I tell you, if anyone steadfastly believes in Me, he will himself be able to do the things that I do; and he will do even greater things than these, because I go to the Father.*
>
> *And I will do [I Myself will grant] whatever you ask in My Name [as presenting all that I AM], so that the Father may be glorified and extolled in (through) the Son.*

[Yes] I will grant [I Myself will do for you] whatever you shall ask in My Name [as presenting all that I AM].

If you [really] love Me, you will keep (obey) My commands.

And I will ask the Father, and He will give you another Comforter (Counselor, Helper, Intercessor, Advocate, Strengthener, and Standby), that He may remain with you forever—

The Spirit of Truth, Whom the world cannot receive (welcome, take to its heart), because it does not see Him or know and recognize Him. But you know and recognize Him, for He lives with you [constantly] and will be in you.

I will not leave you as orphans [comfortless, desolate, bereaved, forlorn, helpless]; I will come [back] to you. (John 14:7–18)

These verses are clear. Jesus states the fact that He and the Father are the same. Further, Jesus says God gives the Spirit of truth and then follows by saying, *I will come to you.* He confirms that He is also the Spirit; He who comes is He who is given. Hence, God is *One* although He manifests Himself as three entities.

Therefore, in Genesis, the meaning of *Us* is God the Father, God the Holy Spirit, and God the Son. The conclusion is Jesus is God the Father and Jesus is God the Holy Spirit.

Although impossible to fully understand, by looking at ourselves, we can get a sense of how this works. God's design for humans was the same as Himself—in His image (Genesis 1:27)—a soul, made in the image of God the Father; a body, made in the image of God the Son; and a spirit, made in the image of the Holy Spirit. My human body is visible and is named Larry Massa. My soul is invisible but will eternally be Larry Massa. My born-again spirit is invisible but is eternally linked to Jesus manifested as the Holy Spirit.

Where self-examination breaks down in attempting to understand what this antinomy is, my body, soul, and spirit cannot be exhibited separately. But throughout the Bible, God is displayed in three parts. Consider when Jesus went to John to be baptized.

"And when Jesus was baptized, He went up at once out of the water; and behold, the heavens were opened, and he [John] saw the Spirit of God descending like a dove and alighting on Him.

And behold, a voice from heaven said, This is My Son, My Beloved, in Whom I delight!" (Matthew 3:16–17).

Here, it appears that *God 1* came up out of the water while *God 2* descended as a dove, then *God 3* spoke from heaven. Let me be clear; there is only God, and He is *One*. The reason God is presented this way is so humans with finite minds can partially understand how God operates within His creation, thus creating the antinomy. Consider John 3:16.

"For God so greatly loved and dearly prized the world that He [even] gave up His only begotten (unique) Son, so that whoever believes in (trusts in, clings to, relies on) Him shall not perish (come to destruction, be lost) but have eternal (everlasting) life" (John 3:16).

This is a remarkable verse and probably the most memorized one in the Bible. It is completely understandable to unbelievers, pre-believers, and immature believers. However, to them, the verse implies that *God 1* gave His Son (*God 2*) so that anyone who believes will gain eternal life through *God 3*.

The mature Christian knows the verse is actually saying God so loved the world that He came in human form and died in human form to atone for mankind's sins so that anyone who believes He actually did do that will have God come into him in spiritual form, thus allowing that person to live forever.

Technically speaking, there actually is no *Son* of God; rather, simply God in human form. In fact, Jesus never referred to Himself as the *Son of God*. He did, however, say He was the *Son of Man* eighty times in the Bible.

Before leaving the mystery of this antinomy, do not form too small an understanding of God (Jesus). He is capable of manifesting Himself as three, but He is beyond our ability to begin to understand His other complexities. Consider He holds together all atoms, so His entire creation does not disintegrate.

He knows every person ever born and is intimately connected to every Christian alive or whose body has previously died. He knows the number of hairs on every head and the number of feathers on every bird.

Yet He handles all this (as displayed in scriptures about Jesus) leisurely. Jesus knew He only had three years to accomplish His mission, but He never appeared to be in a hurry; He leisurely spread His message. Jesus even peacefully slept in a boat that was enduring a tremendous storm.

This is how God deals with His creation now; relaxed, with ease, in control, never stressed, never in a hurry, and always with loving grace.

Do not let your vision of God be too small.

*

MYSTERY 2

Did God Really Abandon
Jesus on the Cross?

Misunderstanding the antinomy of God being One but manifested as three often leads to strange teachings. One most profoundly incorrect is when people attempt to explain why God apparently abandoned Jesus when He was on the cross.

"And at the ninth hour Jesus cried with a loud voice, Eloi, Eloi, lama sabachthani?—which means, My God, My God, why have You forsaken Me [deserting Me and leaving Me helpless and abandoned]?" (Mark 15:34).

I have heard multiple ministers give sermons explaining why Jesus made that statement. The gist of most of them center on the Bible saying anyone hung on a tree is cursed.

"His body shall not remain all night upon the tree, but you shall surely bury him on the same day, for a hanged man is accursed by God. Thus you shall not defile your land which the Lord your God gives you for an inheritance" (Deuteronomy 21:23).

They continue by saying even though Jesus never sinned, He was cursed because He sinned by hanging on a tree. Since God is pure and holy, He had to temporarily leave Jesus because He could not be in Jesus, a sinner. That separation, they claim, caused Jesus to cry out.

Examine how incredibly incorrect such a course of logic is. In the preceding "Mystery," it was shown that Jesus is God. Even though a recent popular book and movie *The Shack* visually showed God as three distinct individuals, there is only *one* God (Deuteronomy 6:4). It makes no sense to think God separated from Himself; how could He?

It is crucial to fully appreciate what God was doing with the crucifixion. As the Bible says, anyone who hangs on a tree is cursed. But understand what the curse is.

"For our sake He made Christ [virtually] to be sin Who knew no sin, so that in and through Him we might become [endued with, viewed as being in, and examples of] the righteousness of God [what we ought to be, approved and acceptable and in right relationship with Him, by His goodness]" (2 Corinthians 5:21).

Jesus did *not* become a sinner; He became *sin*. Since He was made *sin* (everyone's sin was placed on Him—past, present, and future), there was no separation from Himself; God in human form only had to die. By dying, the just penalty for everyone's transgressions was paid in full.

That penalty is God's *all-just* requirement; when someone does something wrong, somebody must *pay*. Mankind had no way to pay for the wrongs they committed (sins). So God was the one who paid as His human form died. Justice would be served, and people could then again be in full fellowship with Him.

Now back to what Jesus said on the cross. In those days, there were almost no books. Each synagogue had a few scrolls, but the general population did not have access to them. In order to teach people and have them internalize lessons from the scrolls, they memorized much, if not all, of the words and stories. Likely, the Psalms were the easiest to memorize because they were mostly songs.

Open your Bible to our most popular Psalm, number 23. Perhaps many of you have memorized it. Now read the Psalm preceding it—number 22. It is a song about a man dying during the crucifixion. It begins, *"My God, My God, why have you forsaken me?..."*

Seriously, read it all. The man speaks of people mocking him: his bones are coming out of his joints, his hands and feet are pierced, they cast lots for his clothing, etc. And it ends with, "*It is finished.*" It is a song about a man who was crucified and is dying.

Perhaps Jesus recited the entire Psalm and only the first and last verses are recorded in the Bible, but even if He didn't, all the Jews standing around would instantly have it come to their minds.

Jesus wasn't railing at God for abandoning Him; He was giving a final sermon to the Jewish people. After rehearsing the song in their minds, they would naturally continue to the Twenty-third Psalm and remember.

"Yes, though I walk through the [deep, sunless] valley of the shadow of death, I will fear or dread no evil, for You are with me; Your rod [to protect] and Your staff [to guide], they comfort me" (Psalm 23:4).

MYSTERY 3

What Did Jesus Look Like?

There are images of Jesus that can be purchased almost anywhere. Most are a "department store" version—long white robe, white skin with a nicely trimmed beard, and long, flowing hair down to His shoulders.

Most certainly He did not have long hair. He was a carpenter. Long hair would constantly get in the way as He leaned over to build things. In addition to that, Apostle Paul wrote that long hair was inappropriate for men.

"Does not the native sense of propriety (experience, common sense, reason) itself teach you that for a man to wear long hair is a dishonor [humiliating and degrading] to him" (1 Corinthians 11:14).

He did not have long hair, but what does the Bible say about His appearance? The only direct evidence of how Jesus looked is the following:

> *"For [the Servant of God] grew up before Him like a tender plant, and like a root out of dry ground; He has no form or comeliness [royal, kingly pomp], that we should look at Him, and no beauty that we should desire Him" (Isaiah 53:2).*

He appeared as just an ordinary man. Nothing of his looks made Him stand out. But He did not have freckles, moles, or any other blemishes on His body.

"But [you were purchased] with the precious blood of Christ (the Messiah), like that of a [sacrificial] lamb without blemish or spot" (1 Peter 1:19).

There is an image, however, of the front and back of a naked man who had been crucified. It is on a linen cloth (a shroud) that has long been thought to be the burial linen of Jesus. The historical recorded dates of the Shroud are:

- AD 525: The Shroud was found in a wall of Edessa above a city gate during a repelled Persian invasion.
- AD 943: The Byzantine army captured Edessa and took the Shroud to Constantinople.
- AD 1204: French crusaders looted Constantinople and took the Shroud.
- AD 1355: The Shroud was displayed in Lirey, France, by Templar Knight Geoffrey de Chamy.
- AD 1532: A fire in a Chambery church housing the Shroud did minor damage to it.
- AD 1534: Nuns attached a full-size support cloth on the back of the Shroud.
- AD 1578: The Shroud was moved to Turin, Italy.

It remains there to this day.

There is a great controversy now centering on whether or not the image is of Jesus. When Jesus was entombed, His body was placed on a linen cloth that was large enough to have His entire body laid on it and then have it folded over Him to completely cover Him. Jesus was resurrected in a way the linen remained folded, but the body disappeared.

"And stooping down, he saw the linen cloths lying there, but he did not enter.

Then Simon Peter came up, following him, and went into the tomb and saw the linen cloths lying there" (John 20:5–6).

There has never been a resurrection since, so no comparatives can be made. There are, however, a large number of small facts providing support for the conclusion that the Shroud of Turin has the image of Jesus:

1. The blood on the linen (proven to be of a human male) was present before the image was made. What artist could make a picture around the existing blood?

2. The image was not painted on. It was formed from a *fading* process similar to how the sun formerly turned drapes hanging in windows yellow over time before UV-protective glass was invented. The process used on the image resulted in different *shades* of yellow fading, generating contrasts that resulted in the complete image of a man. What artist would/could use such a technique?

3. The image on half the linen is of the front part of the man; the other half is his back. When folded, they form a perfect alignment of the two halves to form a single person. Even the most precise artist would have difficulty in accomplishing this.

4. The image has been subjected to several computer analyses which all agree it is three-dimensional. This would be hugely difficult for any skilled artist.

5. The most telling oddity about the image is that it is a *negative*.

Let me explain to those who only take pictures with *point-and-click* cameras or cell phones. Those devices produce pictures that are digital, which means they are numeric representations (in a computer) forming a two-dimensional image.

Nondigital cameras use a film that is very sensitive to light. When a picture is taken, a shutter opens for a brief moment. The most light entering from the image makes the film the darkest; the least light entering does not expose the film as much, so it is lighter. The result is called a *negative*.

In order to see the picture as it originally was taken, a photographic process (called developing the film) is used. This process changes the dark parts back to lighter ones and the lighter parts to darker, completing the original view of the object photographed.

The image on the Shroud is a *negative* just like the films in non-digital cameras. What artist would know how to do that earlier than AD 525? But even if they did, why would they use that technique to generate the image on the linen?

Therefore, to see what Jesus looked like, photograph the image of the Shroud of Turin with a camera with film. Look at the negative on the film *before* developing it. That will be a positive image of Jesus.

There is no record about the Shroud between the resurrection morning and when it was found in Edessa in AD 525. However, it is likely Peter took it from the tomb.

"But Peter got up and ran to the tomb; and stooping down and looking in, he saw the linen cloths alone by themselves, and he went away, wondering about and marveling at what had happened" (Luke 24:12).

Peter looked in the tomb and saw the linens in the early dawn. But shortly after the sun had risen, some women came and encountered a young man who offered to show the women where He had laid.

"And he said to them, Do not be amazed and terrified; you are looking for Jesus of Nazareth, Who was crucified. He has risen; He is not here. See the place where they laid Him" (Mark 16:6).

If the linen was still there, the women would have immediately known where Jesus had been laid; there would be no need for someone to show them.

MYSTERY 9

Why Did Jesus Come to Earth?

As stated in "Mystery 1," mankind's dilemma is there was nothing fallen people could do to be reconciled to God. They had no way to regain fellowship with Him because they had no spirits. They were unable to pay (atone) for their condition and restore a connection with God.

However, the Lord always had a plan to solve humanity's predicament if they, indeed, sinned. Jesus provided the details of it when Nicodemus came to question Him one night:

> *Jesus answered him, I assure you, most solemnly I tell you, that unless a person is born again (anew, from above), he cannot ever see (know, be acquainted with, and experience) the kingdom of God.*
>
> *Nicodemus said to Him, How can a man be born when he is old? Can he enter his mother's womb again and be born?*
>
> *Jesus answered, I assure you, most solemnly I tell you, unless a man is born of water and [even] the Spirit, he cannot [ever] enter the kingdom of God.*
>
> *What is born of [from] the flesh is flesh [of the physical is physical]; and what is born of the Spirit is spirit. (John 3:3–6)*

Jesus knew exactly why Nicodemus had come, so He immediately told him that without being born anew, Nicodemus could never experience the kingdom of God. What Jesus was teaching was that mankind must obtain a spirit—be born again.

Every person coming into existence after the sin of Adam was his descendant. This means their soul and mortal body followed in his lineage. But unfortunately, since Adam's spirit had died, mankind did not inherit a spirit.

Jesus was the exception because He (as God the Father) caused Himself to become human, not as a descendant of Adam (after he sinned) with no spirit, but as a human with a live spirit (the Holy Spirit).

This made Jesus sinless and allowed Him to be the only substitute for mankind able to satisfy God's perfect justice: man had disobeyed, so someone sinless had to pay.

Jesus's death and resurrection allowed every person to have their spirits newly born when they accepted His undeserved gift. Jesus told Nicodemus the only way his spirit could be reborn was to believe in Him.

"In order that everyone who believes in Him [who cleaves to Him, trusts Him, and relies on Him] may not perish, but have eternal life and [actually] live forever! "...that whoever believes in Him should not perish but have eternal life" (John 3:15).

Often the word *on* is used after the word *believe* because the Greek word *pisteuo* has no single English word for translation. To *believe in* someone is a passive verb. It is like saying one believes in Abraham Lincoln.

However, the best translation of the word *believes* in John 3:16 has an active meaning. Its correct interpretation is *to trust in, rely on, and adhere to* Jesus's sacrifice to make a person whole (receive a newly born spirit) and to obtain eternal life.

Jesus's purpose for coming to earth was to not only show how a person should live during their life on earth but to also provide a way for them to obtain a spirit so their soul could be in eternal fellowship with God again.

MYSTERY 5

Why Do the Gospel Resurrection Accounts Differ Widely?

The most important event in the Bible is the resurrection of Jesus. Without His resurrection from the dead, there would be no hope. The entire Bible would be valueless, empty of life. The Apostle Paul put it this way.

"If we who are [abiding] in Christ have hope only in this life and that is all, then we are of all people most miserable and to be pitied" (1 Corinthians 15:19).

But He was resurrected. The accounts described in the four Gospels, however, are so different some have problems believing there actually was a resurrection. The four versions appear to be hopelessly contradictory.

Others, in an attempt to defend the differences, suggest they were written by four different men describing the same event from four different viewpoints. They claim the differences underscore the truth of the story.

Pointing to the description of a car wreck as an illustration, if four people's stories were exactly the same, they would appear to have colluded about the narrative, thus making it suspicious.

The problem with this theory is the Bible is the inspired Word of God. There is no way He would allow only one of the accounts to be true while the others were false. There are no contradictions in the Bible.

Consider the key elements of the four Gospel statements to understand the basic differences from one to another.

Matthew 28:1–10

1. Mary of Magdala and the other Mary visited the tomb.
2. An angel removed the stone from the opening.
3. The guards fainted.
4. The angel told the women to not be afraid; Jesus had risen.
5. The women left with fear and great joy, met Jesus on the way, and clasped His feet.
6. Jesus instructed them to tell the brethren to go to Galilee, and He would see them there.

Mark 16:1–11

1. After the Sabbath ended, Mary Magdalene, Mary (James's mother), and Salome bought spices to anoint Jesus's body.
2. Some women went to the tomb and wondered how they would be able to open it.
3. Upon arrival, they saw the stone had been rolled back unsealing it.
4. They went into the tomb and found a single man. He told them Jesus had risen and told them to tell the disciples to go to Galilee.
5. They ran from the tomb, terrified, and said nothing of the encounter to anyone.

Luke 24:1–12

1. Women with spices found the tomb open, went in, and were perplexed that Jesus's body was gone.
2. Two men suddenly appeared, frightening the women.
3. The men said Jesus had risen and reminded them He had earlier instructed about what would happen.

4.   The women were Mary Magdalene, Joanna, James's mother, and some other women.
5.   They went to where the disciples were staying and reported their experience to them.
6.   Peter ran to the tomb alone, looked in, and saw the linens.

John 20:1–18

1.   Mary Magdalene went alone to the tomb and saw it was open.
2.   Without looking in, she ran to where Peter and John were staying.
3.   All three returned to the tomb; John (the fastest) arrived first. Peter quickly followed, and Mary was far behind.
4.   John looked in and saw the burial cloth.
5.   Peter went into the tomb and saw the linens.
6.   John entered and believed Jesus had been resurrected.
7.   Both went back to their lodgings.
8.   Mary finally arrived again at the tomb, looked in, and saw two angels.
9.   She turned from the tomb, saw Jesus, but didn't recognize Him until He said her name.
10. Mary then knew Him by sight, but He told her to not cling to Him, for He had not yet ascended to the Father.
11. She ran to the disciples and told them she had just seen Jesus.

Although the accounts do appear to contradict each other, there is a simple fact that will harmonize all four. But before proceeding to it, there are two subtleties that must be understood. The first is Matthew's writing style. Consider Matthew 2:7–16, how he describes the wise men finding Jesus:

> *Then Herod sent for the wise men [astrologers]*
> *secretly, and accurately to the last point ascertained*

from them the time of the appearing of the star [that is, how long the star had made itself visible since its rising in the east].

Then he sent them to Bethlehem, saying, Go and search for the Child carefully and diligently, and when you have found Him, bring me word, that I too may come and worship Him.

When they had listened to the king, they went their way, and behold, the star which had been seen in the east in its rising went before them until it came and stood over the place where the young Child was.

When they saw the star, they were thrilled with ecstatic joy.

And on going into the house, they saw the Child with Mary His mother, and they fell down and worshiped Him. Then opening their treasure bags, they presented to Him gifts—gold and frankincense and myrrh.

And [receiving an answer to their asking, they were divinely instructed and warned in a dream not to go back to Herod; so they departed to their own country by a different way.

Now after they had gone, behold, an angel of the Lord appeared to Joseph in a dream and said, Get up! [Tenderly] take unto you the young Child and His mother and flee to Egypt; and remain there till I tell you [otherwise], for Herod intends to search for the Child in order to destroy Him.

And having risen, he took the Child and His mother by night and withdrew to Egypt

And remained there until Herod's death. This was to fulfill what the Lord had spoken by the prophet, Out of Egypt have I called My Son.

Then Herod, when he realized that he had been misled by the wise men, was furiously enraged, and he sent and put to death all the male children in Bethlehem and in all that territory who were two years old and under, reckoning according to the date which he had investigated diligently and had learned exactly from the wise men. (Matthew 2:7–16)

Note how he writes that Herod sent the wise men to Bethlehem. In verse 12, Matthew describes that the wise men were told in a dream to not return to Herod. However, in verses 13–15, he interrupts his narrative timeline of what Herod did in order to describe how Joseph was warned in a dream to take Jesus to Egypt and remain there until Herod died.

Then, in verse 16, Matthew again picks up the original narrative timeline by saying Herod realized he had been deceived by the wise men and sent soldiers to kill all males in Bethlehem, two years of age and under.

In like matter, Matthew interrupts his narrative timeline of the tomb visit in chapter 28 between verses 1 and 2.

"Now after the Sabbath, as the first day of the week began to dawn Mary Magdalene and the other Mary came to see the tomb" (Matthew 28:1).

The pause is done so Matthew could explain how the tomb was opened.

"And behold, there was a great earthquake; for an angel of the Lord descended from heaven, and came and rolled back the stone from the door, and sat on it. His countenance was like lightning and his clothing as white as snow. And the guards shook for fear of him, and became like dead men" (Matthew 28:2–4).

Completing his explanation, he returns to the story timeline in verse 5.

"But the angel answered and said to the women, "Do not be afraid, for I know that you seek Jesus who was crucified" (Matthew 28:5).

If Matthew were writing this with today's methods, verses 2–4 would be in parentheses, just as the explanation about Joseph going to Egypt would have been.

The conclusion is, time-wise, the tomb was clearly open long before anyone arrived that first day of the week. It was opened not to let Jesus out, but to allow those coming to go in.

The second subtle point to understand is how biblical days and nights were measured, which creates a time gap between Mark 11:1 and 2.

In verse 1, Mark states that Mary Magdalene and Salome bought spices after the Sabbath ended because the markets would be closed until then. The Jews reckoned time as a day started at dark and ended at dark, twenty-four hours later.

Good Friday started at about 6:00 p.m. Thursday and ended at 6:00 p.m. Friday. The Sabbath started at 6:00 p.m. Friday and ended at 6:00 p.m. Saturday. The first day of the week (when the tomb was discovered empty at dawn) began at 6:00 p.m. Saturday and ended at 6:00 p.m. Sunday.

Therefore, Mary Magdalene and Salome bought spices Saturday evening after 6:00 p.m. when people could legally sell things. But since it was dark, they would not venture to the tomb until first light—after the night hours. This means the time interval between verses 1 and 2 is somewhere between eight to ten hours.

Lastly, it is interesting to note who are not mentioned in any of the Gospel resurrection accounts. Mary, mother of Jesus, is not there. And Mary and Martha (Lazarus's sisters) are not there either.

Therefore, it is reasonable to assume Mary (mother of Jesus) was so distraught after the crucifixion that she was staying at Lazarus's house in Bethany.

It also is reasonable to assume John would be staying there, too, for Jesus told John he was to care for His mother (John 19:27). But that night (of the first day of the week), John was certainly with the other disciples in the Upper Room (Acts 1:13).

Unraveling the resurrection accounts starts with the understanding living was much more difficult in biblical days than today. Obtaining food, cooking meals, and washing clothes were difficult, time-consuming events. In order to allow Jesus and His disciples sufficient time to teach and preach the Gospel, numerous women accompanied them to minister to them.

"Many women were there, watching from a distance. They had followed Jesus from Galilee to care for his needs" (Matthew 27:55 NIV).

Mary Magdalene was the leader of this band of women.

Therefore, the resurrection story really starts in Matthew 27:61. Mary Magdalene and Mary (mother of James and Joseph) were sitting opposite the tomb, watching Joseph of Arimathea wrap Jesus's body in a linen cloth (Matthew 27:59).

In biblical times, only men could prepare men's bodies for burial, but women could do both sexes. Since Joseph was a rich man, it is unlikely he had fixed many bodies for burial, if any at all.

Mary Magdalene did not think Joseph was doing a good job preparing the body. She left before Nicodemus arrived with spices (John 19:39–40).

She organized the other women to meet early the morning after the night the Sabbath ended, and they would all go to the tomb to properly bury Jesus. But Mary Magdalene had to wait until after the Sabbath ended to obtain the things she wanted to use for His burial.

A quick check of the times provided by the Bible reveals the four Gospel accounts are *not* describing the same event four times, but four different ones occurring at four different times on that resurrection morning. Those times are in reverse order of the four Gospels.

John 20:1–18

John's Gospel provides the first visit by stating Mary Magdalene went to the tomb *while it was still dark.* She found out the High Priest had arranged for the tomb to be guarded and decided to use her womanly wiles (her former profession was a prostitute) to distract them so the others could properly prepare the body. She went to the tomb alone while it was still dark.

The guards had already seen the tomb being opened by an earthquake and that it was empty, so they had left to tell the High Priest about what had happened.

Mary saw the tomb was open but didn't even look in. She quickly concluded someone had stolen the body.

Mary ran to the Upper Room and awakened Peter (John was there, heard Mary, and also woke up) to tell him someone stole the body. She used a particular technique to add credibility to her statement.

That is, rather than use the singular person, she used a plural form (John 20:2). This gives force to the statement. She had just awakened two people with the incredible statement, "We do not know where they laid Him," when in fact she was the only one who did not know.

Peter and John believed her enough to investigate. They both took off sprinting, greatly outdistancing Mary. John was the young one, so he arrived at the tomb first and looked in. It was still dark, so even though he could see the burial wrappings, he did not get the full impact of the sight.

Peter arrived, grabbed a burning stick from the guard's fire for light, and immediately went in. John followed him and saw an extraordinary sight.

When people were entombed during those days, the head had small linen strips wrapped around and around about it. The final action was a long, linen cloth was placed under the body, then folded over the top, much like a blanket.

Peter and John saw the folded linen with no body under it. But Jesus had made sure the small linen strips wrapped around His head were no longer under the folded *blanket* but were in a different place. The wrappings were untouched with no head inside. This sight would make it clear the body had disappeared from within miraculously, not stolen.

They decided to tell Mary, mother of Jesus, about the empty tomb and began walking toward Bethany, a different route than what Mary would be using to go back to the tomb. After a while, Peter decided to let John relate the story alone, and they both went back to where they had been lodging, Peter to the Upper Room, John to Bethany.

Finally, after Peter and John had left, Mary arrived back at the tomb. She looked into it and saw two angels who asked why she was crying. As she answered, she saw another man. She did not recognize Him, either because she was sobbing or because Jesus had made His body unrecognizable as He did with the two men on the road to Emmaus (Luke 24:17–31).

When Mary finally recognized Jesus, He told her to not cling to Him, for He had not yet ascended to the Father. He also instructed her to tell the disciples He was going to the Father immediately.

She ran back to the Upper Room to tell the disciples she had seen Jesus alive.

Luke 24:1–12

The Bible moves the account a little farther in time and states *it was early dawn (right before sunrise).* James's mother, Joanna, and some other women had met at the proper place with the spices at the time agreed upon. Mary Magdalene was not there (as well as a subset of other women), but they knew she was going early to occupy the guards. So they went to the tomb.

Upon arriving, they found it open, went inside, and saw Jesus's body was gone. Their purpose was to properly prepare the body, but it was not there. As they tried to decide what to do, two men (they could have been angels, for angels had appeared to people in the Old Testament as men [Genesis 19:2 and 5]) suddenly stood by them.

They told the women Jesus had risen and instructed them to tell the disciples to go to Galilee to see Him. The women ran off to where the disciples were (the Upper Room), arriving shortly after Mary Magdalene had returned from seeing Jesus. They all described what happened and Mary Magdalene even told them she saw Jesus alive.

None of the disciples believed the women, but Peter (John had gone to Bethany) went back to the tomb a second time by himself hoping to encounter Jesus. However, he looked in and saw the linen cloths just as they were the first time. He left marveling at what had happened and what he had heard (Luke 24:10–12).

Mark 16:1–11

Now the Bible says it is *after the sun had risen.* The remainder of the women who had agreed to meet at the designated location arrived late. They knew they were late, assumed the others had gone to the tomb, and decided to go by themselves.

The original plan involved enough women to be able to remove the stone cover. However, the number of this last set of women was so small that they wondered if they would be able to move it if needed.

When they arrived, however, the tomb was open. They went inside and encountered a single young man. They were so startled by a living person being there they bolted and ran away from the tomb terrified.

The young man was probably yelling at them as they ran away and told them to tell the disciples to go to Galilee. This group of women was so frightened they said nothing about the encounter to anyone.

Matthew 28:1–10

The timeline ends when Mary Magdalene and James's mother decided to go back to the tomb together. They each had already seen it separately, but it is easy to understand why they would like to revisit it.

The Bible sets the time as *near dawn* which can be right before or right after dawn. Therefore, right after dawn, the sun had risen; daylight abounded.

Note the Bible states the two went to *take a look at the tomb*— not to take spices, for they already knew Jesus had risen. When they arrived, they saw a single angel sitting on the tombstone.

He told them Jesus had risen, offered them to look in the tomb, and directed them to tell the disciples He would be in Galilee. They left hastily (without looking in the tomb; they already knew it was empty) with fear *and great joy* for they were finally beginning to realize what happened that morning.

They didn't go far until Jesus met them. He, by then, had ascended to His Father and returned. When the two clasped his feet, He allowed it. This time He told them to tell the brethren to go to Galilee to see Him there.

In conclusion, this harmonization explains away every apparent contradiction in the four Gospel accounts in a logical manner. The Bible remains corroborated.

MYSTERY 6

Love

The English language is sometimes difficult to understand because too many words have multiple definitions; the context of its use is then often required to know which definition is intended. Sometimes, the context is not really enough.

An example is "man is the head of his wife." There are about thirty definitions of the word *head*. There is no real context, so people choose from the many possible definitions the one they want; most pick *leader*. The word translated *head* in the Bible really means *source* (headwaters).

Another word in the Bible people misunderstand is the word *love*. People usually think *love* means an intense deep affection when used as a noun; feel a deep affection for someone when used as a verb.

The New Testament is translated to English from Greek. There are seven different words in Greek that can be translated as *love* in English, but all have distinctly different meanings:

1. *Eros*—romantic, passionate love
2. *Philia*—intimate, authentic friendship
3. *Ludus*—playful, flirtatious love
4. *Storge*—unconditional, familial love
5. *Philautia*—self-love
6. *Pragma*—committed, companionate love
7. *Agápe*—empathetic, unconditional, universal love

The mystery of *love* is trying to understand those different meanings when simply translated *love* in most Bibles. In John 21, it appears that Jesus asks Peter if he loves Him three times—in the same manner. Of course, Jesus is allowing Peter to erase his three denials before the crucifixion, but there is something deeper that Jesus does.

Here, the *Amplified Bible* clearly differentiates the meaning of the word *love*:

> *When they had eaten, Jesus said to Simon Peter, Simon, son of John, do you love Me more than these [others do—with reasoning, intentional, spiritual devotion, as one loves the Father]? He said to Him, Yes, Lord, You know that I love You [that I have deep, instinctive, personal affection for You, as for a close friend]. He said to him, Feed My lambs.*
>
> *Again He said to him the second time, Simon, son of John, do you love Me [with reasoning, intentional, spiritual devotion, as one loves the Father]? He said to Him, Yes, Lord, You know that I love You [that I have a deep, instinctive, personal affection for You, as for a close friend]. He said to him, Shepherd (tend) My sheep.*
>
> *He said to him the third time, Simon, son of John, do you love Me [with a deep, instinctive, personal affection for Me, as for a close friend]? Peter was grieved (was saddened and hurt) that He should ask him the third time, Do you love Me? And he said to Him, Lord, You know everything; You know that I love You [that I have a deep, instinctive, personal affection for You, as for a close friend]. Jesus said to him, Feed My sheep. (John 21:15–17)*

Jesus asks Peter the first time if he *agape* loves Him; Peter answers he *philia* loves Him. Jesus asks the same question again, and Peter answers the same way the second time. But Jesus asks Peter the third time if he *philia* loves Him. Jesus went to Peter's level. He was willing to *meet* Peter in the same language describing where Peter was emotionally.

God often does this, and we are blessed when He does. He tries to bring us to a higher level, but when we are unable, He comes to ours.

Love needs to be understood in the seven definitions from the Greek ones, but it is clear Jesus's new commandment is *agape* love, the way Jesus loved them.

"I give you a new commandment: that you should love one another. Just as I have loved you, so you too should love one another" (John 13:34).

With this knowledge, the nature of love can better be understood. It is best described by Paul's description of love in 1 Corinthians 13:

> *Even if I dole out all that I have [to the poor in providing] food, and if I surrender my body to be burned or in order that I may glory, but have not love (God's love in me), I gain nothing.*
>
> *Love endures long and is patient and kind; love never is envious nor boils over with jealousy, is not boastful or vainglorious, does not display itself haughtily.*
>
> *It is not conceited (arrogant and inflated with pride); it is not rude (unmannerly) and does not act unbecomingly. Love (God's love in us) does not insist on its own rights or its own way, for it is not self-seeking; it is not touchy or fretful or resentful; it takes no account of the evil done to it [it pays no attention to a suffered wrong].*
>
> *It does not rejoice at injustice and unrighteousness, but rejoices when right and truth prevail.*
>
> *Love bears up under anything and everything that comes, is ever ready to believe the best of every person, its hopes are fadeless under all circumstances, and it endures everything [without weakening]. (1 Corinthians 13:3–7)*

It is clear love here is God's love, *agape* love, or unconditional love. Not only do these verses describe the nature of love, but they also describe the nature of God. Simply read those verses again and replace the word *love* with the word *God*—God is love.

MYSTERY 7

Life

At first thought, life does not seem like a biblical mystery at all. Everyone who reads this book is alive and did not need the Bible to know it. The biblical mystery, however, is being alive; and reading this book is not the whole story. Genesis says we are made in God's image.

"God said, Let Us [Father, Son, and Holy Spirit] make mankind in Our image, after Our likeness" (Genesis 1:26).

If we are created in the image of God, our *life* must be like God. It must have a soul (like God the Father), a body (like God the Son), and a spirit (like God the Holy Spirit). And that is the mystery.

It is clear when a man and woman procreate, a sperm enters an egg, and a new *life* begins. What is obscure is when that happens, a human soul is delivered from heaven and enters into the human body.

"Before I formed you in the womb I knew [and] approved of you [as My chosen instrument], and before you were born I separated and set you apart, consecrating you; [and] I appointed you as a prophet to the nations" (Jeremiah 1:5).

God creates a *soul* in heaven and an angel transmits it into the fertilized egg in the womb of a woman. The result is a human being begins to grow, body and soul. At birth, that human enters into God's created world and begins to mature.

As pointed out in "Mystery 4," the problem is, although we were to be made in the image of God, at birth we are only two-thirds of the image. Because Adam sinned, everyone inherits an existence without a spirit. This fact results in a person being able to choose to become fully in the image of God or to remain simply as born.

This decision dictates the future of one's life. The soul is God-made and never ceases to exist. When the body dies, the soul will either enter Hades (the place God created for souls to temporarily abide) or go directly to heaven.

From "Mystery 4," the way to make that choice is quite simple; acknowledge Jesus died for your sins (past, present, and future). Trust He forgives your past sins, rely on Him to continue to forgive your future ones, and stick to that belief always; in short, believe on Him. It is totally a matter of having faith. Nothing other than believing on Jesus is necessary.

Once you have done that, your spirit is born; you become complete in the image of God. God's spirit connects with your newly born spirit, and He never leaves you. Do not miss the impact of God coming to live inside you; your spirit is connected to His Spirit.

You will never be alone again; He is always with you. You will always be loved unconditionally by Him. Life will continue to be challenging, and bad things will occasionally happen. But you always will have Him to lean on; He will never leave you. Best of all, you will go to heaven when your mortal body dies.

More will be said about death in "Mystery 8," but there was a popular radio commentator, Paul Harvey, who described the best way to think about bodily death. His story went something like this.

Suppose all the babies in the wombs of every pregnant woman could talk to one another on a telephone. The day Jonny's mother gave birth, they would all get on the phone and say, "Poor old Jonny just passed away."

Once one goes to heaven, the adventure really begins. Souls project an image of one's mortal body. People recognize one another, can interact with others, and can touch others.

But when the church age ends, the real fun begins. Everyone in heaven and all Christians alive on earth will be collected together at a particular moment (called the Rapture) and be given an immortal body. This is done in preparation for their returning to earth with Jesus at His Second Coming.

A *glorified* body will be able to do all the things Jesus could do after He received one. One can *will* their way to any location instantly and be fully clothed. The body can eat and is solid to touch. It can be recognized or not (Luke 24).

Believers will remain in heaven for seven years after the Rapture while the Israel age is completed. During those seven years, people who accept Jesus's salvation and are killed (saints) will join Christians in heaven, be given glorified bodies, and will also accompany Jesus when He returns to earth at the end of the tribulation period. Both believers and saints will judge the people of earth for one thousand years:

> *Then I saw thrones, and sitting on them were those to whom authority to act as judges and to pass sentence was entrusted. Also I saw the souls of those who had been slain with axes [beheaded] for their witnessing to Jesus and [for preaching and testifying] for the Word of God, and who had refused to pay homage to the beast or his statue and had not accepted his mark or permitted it to be stamped on their foreheads or on their hands. And they lived again and ruled with Christ (the Messiah) a thousand years. (Revelation 20:4).*

The evil forces will be overcome by Jesus, and Satan will be put into prison for a thousand years.

Being a judge will require unique abilities which hinge on the spiritual gifts given individually during their mortal body's life on earth. They will have a big job to do for the earth will be in miserable shape at the end of the tribulation period.

All water will be blood-filled. Everything in the sea will have perished. Most of the vegetation will be burned up. The earth's contour will be changed; there will be no mountains. Many rivers will be dried up. Check Revelation 16 for complete details.

The consequence of all this will be the people who survive the tribulation and who are allowed to enter into the thousand-year period will have much rebuilding to do.

The restoration of the earth will be done by people living there, but believers will help people decide the best way to accomplish the rebuilding. They will *judge* what are the best ideas to effectively pursue restoration.

This period will be a unique chapter of earth's history, for people will again live for many years (Isaiah 65:20). Animals will coexist without killing one another (check "Mystery 8") because people will have spirits and be able to control animal instincts (Isaiah 11:6–8).

People do die but usually live to be quite old. The period will be somewhat a utopia because the perfect form of government (slavery) will be in place. Jesus will be the ruler (Master) over the whole world.

At the end of the thousand-year period, Jesus and all believers will return to heaven, and Satan will be released from his prison. What happens then is detailed in "Mystery 17." The rest of the mystery of life is also described there.

MYSTERY 8

Death

Death is first mentioned in Genesis when God told Adam to not eat from the *tree of knowledge*. He said if Adam did, he would die. The Hebrew word translated as *surely die* in most Bibles really means *to die, die*. This is correct, for Adam experienced two deaths. The first was instantaneous; his spirit immediately died.

"*Therefore, as sin came into the world through one man, and death as the result of sin, so death spread to all men, [no one being able to stop it or to escape its power] because all men sinned*" (Romans 5:12).

The second is that aging began. That means nothing *aged* to death before Adam sinned. After the sin, everything grew to maturity (as it did before sin) but continued to age until it ultimately died:

> For [even the whole] creation (all nature) waits expectantly and longs earnestly for God's sons to be made known [waits for the revealing, the disclosing of their sonship].
>
> For the creation (nature) was subjected to frailty (to futility, condemned to frustration), not because of some intentional fault on its part, but by the will of Him Who so subjected it—[yet] with the hope
>
> That nature (creation) itself will be set free from its bondage to decay and corruption [and

*gain an entrance] into the glorious freedom of God's
children.*

   *We know that the whole creation [of irrational
creatures] has been moaning together in the pains of
labor until now. (Romans 8:19–22)*

When the mortal body dies and has not chosen to receive a
born-again spirit, that soul remains in Hades until the final judgment. At that judgment, their soul is placed in the lake of fire—the
second death:

   *Then death and Hades (the state of death or
disembodied existence) were thrown into the lake of
fire. This is the second death, the lake of fire.*

   *And if anyone's [name] was not found recorded
in the Book of Life, he was hurled into the lake of
fire. (Revelation 20:14–15)*

These two deaths were never intended to happen when God
created the world; they occurred because of sin. Both are bad, but
with the arrival of sin, a third *death* became good.

   When a person realizes he must accept Jesus's *payment* for his
sins to obtain eternal life, he is motivated to stop sinning. This is
perfectly natural and is commendable for if a person continues in sin,
he will ultimately lose his salvation:

   *For if we go on deliberately and willingly
sinning after once acquiring the knowledge of the
Truth, there is no longer any sacrifice left to atone
for [our] sins [no further offering to which to look
forward].*

   *[There is nothing left for us then] but a kind of
awful and fearful prospect and expectation of divine
judgment and the fury of burning wrath and indig-
nation which will consume those who put themselves in opposition [to God]. (Hebrews 10:26–27)*

The mistake comes with the person deciding he will stop sinning. The greater mistake is when he plans to stop sinning by prioritizing them and starts with the one he thinks is the worst.

For example, suppose it is viewing pornography. The person will focus on not visiting websites that show pornography, not visiting stores selling or renting pornography, etc. But by doing that, he has made Satan's job much easier. The devil only needs to work on tripping up the individual by making sure pornography bombards him. The result—the person will again view pornography.

Before arriving at an approach to not sin and explaining more about this third *death*, the first sin by Adam must be understood completely; it was more than just disobeying a God-given commandment.

"But of the tree of the knowledge of good and evil and blessing and calamity you shall not eat, for in the day that you eat of it you shall surely die" (Genesis 2:17).

The motivation was to be like God.

"For God knows that in the day you eat of it your eyes will be opened, and you will be like God, knowing the difference between good and evil and blessing and calamity" (Genesis 3:5).

Eating the fruit resulted in Adam and Eve knowing both good and evil (not just knowing the difference between good and evil but knowing both). Since they then knew both, they gained autonomy from God; became independent, on their own.

So the problem with deciding to not sin is the same as the sin Adam committed. As one who is autonomous, one decides he will not sin *on his own*—doing it *his way*. There are two problems with this; first, it will not work, and second, it is committing another sin. The dilemma then becomes this: How does one stop?

The key to this is understanding there is a third *death* spoken of in the Bible; it is the death to self:

> We were buried therefore with Him by the baptism into death, so that just as Christ was raised from the dead by the glorious [power] of the Father, so we too might [habitually] live and behave in newness of life.

> *For if we have become one with Him by sharing a death like His, we shall also be [one with Him in sharing] His resurrection [by a new life lived for God].*
>
> *We know that our old (unrenewed) self was nailed to the cross with Him in order that [our] body [which is the instrument] of sin might be made ineffective and inactive for evil, that we might no longer be the slaves of sin.*
>
> *For when a man dies, he is freed (loosed, delivered) from [the power of] sin [among men].*
>
> *Now if we have died with Christ, we believe that we shall also live with Him. (Romans 6:4–8)*

The goal becomes totally dying to self; losing all autonomy. That means one must become a slave; not of captivity, but voluntarily.

Slavery is the perfect form of government if and only if the master is morally perfect. This is why slavery is not necessarily condemned by the Bible. While capturing someone and making them do whatever you want is hideous, voluntarily deciding to become a slave to Jesus and submitting totally to Him is exactly what one needs to do to stop sinning.

"But now since you have been set free from sin and have become the slaves of God, you have your present reward in holiness and its end is eternal life" (Romans 6:22).

One must acknowledge that not only is Jesus our Savior, but He is our Master (Lord).

In my recent book *Indwelt*, I pointed out that when we accept Jesus, we gain a new spirit, but it is a baby one that needs to grow. I further showed how that growth is attained. But the measure of that growth is how much we die to self and how much we surrender our autonomy (will) to Jesus.

The bottom line is this: overcome any and all sin by totally giving up your autonomy (dying to self) and becoming slaves to Jesus. When we do that completely, then He calls us friends, brothers, and finally, Sons of God.

Before leaving the topic of death, there is one more mystery to examine. Some believe there was no death of any kind before Adam committed the first sin. Of course, this is impossible.

When an apple is picked from a tree, it has died (cut off from its life support). When the apple is eaten and the seeds are planted, the seeds die so a new tree can grow. When the inedible core is discarded, it doesn't just lie there forever but decomposes; that is death. The question then becomes what was the extent of death before Adam sinned?

When the earth was teeming with life, animals and people accidentally stepped on bugs or ants killing them. Animals would accidentally fall into the water and die. Some animals would fight for territorial rights and kill in the process.

God instructed mankind to *subdue* the earth and rule over animals and fish (Genesis 1:28). That means man was to *overcome* the natural behavior of all living creatures and subject them to man's control in a specific way.

Animals have no soul or spirit like mankind. They do, however, have a soul-like awareness of themselves and can think a little. Rather than a spirit, God gave them instincts. It is clear God provided a vegetarian diet so all breathing creatures could survive without killing to eat:

> *And God said, See, I have given you every plant yielding seed that is on the face of all the land and every tree with seed in its fruit; you shall have them for food.*
>
> *And to all the animals on the earth and to every bird of the air and to everything that creeps on the ground—to everything in which there is the breath of life—I have given every green plant for food. And it was so. (Genesis 1:29–30)*

But did they only eat plants? God created animals as carnivores, omnivores, or herbivores. They all could survive on a vegetarian diet. However, their instincts would lead them to consume what they wanted.

Mankind could control their behavior by subduing (overcoming) the animal's instincts. They did so through the use of their own spirits. A man's spirit was not only connected to God but could connect with and control animal instincts.

When man was around animals, they would be controlled by him. They could not kill to eat or follow any other instinct unless granted by man's spirit. This control provided a very clear picture of how death would be understood by Adam and Eve.

When animals were not around man's control, their instincts dominated them. Carnivores would kill and eat other animals; omnivores would do so also or simply eat vegetables, fruits, and vegetation.

Carnivores did not just start killing and eating flesh the day Adam sinned. They did it instinctively when not controlled by man's spirit before the fall. When mankind no longer had a spirit, the animal's instincts dominated them, and the behavior we see in them now prevailed.

Further, although fish breathe (take on oxygen), they are not included in God providing vegetation for survival. There are a few fish that can live without eating other fish or living organisms, but it is rare. The bulk eat insects, worms, smaller fish, etc. This results in death. Like animals, fish are self-aware and have instincts that man's spirit could control.

Realize, when God looked at His total creation and declared it was very good (Genesis 1:31), He did not say it because there was no death, but because nature was in perfect balance.

Today, believers who have been given new spirits still cannot dominate the instincts of animals because when Adam sinned, the earth became the domain of Satan. Jesus will reclaim *title deed* to the earth at His Second Coming and then believers will once again use their spirits to dominate the animal's instincts:

> *And the wolf shall dwell with the lamb, and*
> *the leopard shall lie down with the kid, and the calf*
> *and the young lion and the fatted domestic animal*
> *together; and a little child shall lead them.*

And the cow and the bear shall feed side by side, their young shall lie down together, and the lion shall eat straw like the ox. (Isaiah 11:6–7)

Human death will ultimately be destroyed (Revelation 20:14), but animal/plant death (not due to aging) will continue in eternity (see "Mystery 17").

MYSTERY 9

Time

There appears to be no mystery about *time*. We all live in it and have all of our lives. We have somewhat the same notions about it. The qualities of time appear to be intuitive; we pass through it, everyone experiences each moment in time simultaneously, the past has disappeared, the future has not yet happened, and everyone can measure it the same way at any given instant.

The mystery comes about because no one knows what *time* actually is. In the past, I defined it as the measure of increasing entropy (randomness or coming apart). And since we are living during the time after the first sin, that definition is somewhat accurate for we experience age and the disintegration of *closed* systems. However, *time* is much more than that.

As previously stated, the qualities of time we now experience appear to be the same for everyone simultaneously. However, current physics has proven those notions are wrong. One should research such truth, but this book will only examine four aspects of the nature of time; it is affected by speed, distance, gravity, and it is relative.

Einstein's *general relativity* and *special relativity* theories (which have now been proven) have completely changed how we understand the nature of time as we experience it. Consider speed first.

Light travels at a constant rate of 186,000 miles per second. Imagine a *light* clock as a box where in one second a ball of light travels from the bottom to the top. The next second, the ball travels from the top to the bottom. The distance the light traveled horizontally can easily be measured.

Now consider if the box is moved to the right just as the ball of light went from the bottom to the top; the speed of light does not change, but the top of the box is now in a different place. The light ball must move a little farther to the right to hit the top of the box.

The path of light is no longer perfectly horizontal but slanted slightly. That slanted path can be perfectly measured, but the distance is slightly longer. When the box moves rapidly, the distance of the slanting line increases dramatically. That means a second in the moving box is slower than one in the box not moving. The conclusion is as speed increases, time decreases.

Considering the effect of distance on time adds to its mystery. Imagine moments in time are like slices in a loaf of bread. Pick a particular slice (a moment across the entire universe) and everyone existing at that moment experiences the same thing that is happening.

But suppose a person is very far away and begins to slowly move farther away. Their *slice* of time (their *now*) will be different from yours. If they are far enough away and moving farther, their slice of time will include a past moment of your time. If they move closer to you from a far distance, a slice of their time will contain a future moment of your time. So distance affects time.

The mystery deepens with the inclusion of time being affected by gravity. Atomic clocks have been developed that are extremely precise in their measurement of time. When two are located side by side on the earth's surface, they measure time exactly the same.

But when one is taken very high in the earth's atmosphere for a while and then is returned to the earth and placed by the clock that remained, the earth clock measured less time than the one which went to an area of less gravity. The conclusion is as gravity increases, time becomes slower.

Rounding out the mystery of *time*, it is relative to the observer. Suppose you are standing on a small hill watching a train speed by. When the exact midpoint of the train is in front of you, lightning strikes the back and front of the train at the same moment. You see both flashes simultaneously.

However, consider a passenger on the train who was sitting in a seat at the train's midpoint. He would see the front flash at an earlier *moment* than the back lightning flash. The conclusion is time depends upon one's perspective (it is relative).

Having now learned a little about the nature of time, this book will examine the mysteries of time as it delves into the mysteries of heaven, creation, Hades, eternity, and the period before the first sin.

MYSTERY 10

Creation Time

The book of Genesis starts with God creating the heavens and earth. It is interesting that He did not first say, "Let there be time." Rather, He said, "Let there be light." Light can be a visible spectrum or invisible (like radiation). Most likely, the first light was invisible to the human eye.

When God created the sun, moon, and stars, they became sources of light that humans could see. It is most likely (though not necessary) their light traveled at 186,000 miles per second, as now. By creating light traveling over a distance, time was also created.

There is a great controversy over the period God stated it took Him to perform His works of creation. The Hebrew word to describe it is *yom*. It is correctly translated as day. It is the same word as translated in the book of Numbers, chapter 7 verse 1, so people who take the Bible as completely literal maintain that God did His creative acts each in one rotation of the earth.

Those who believe God created the world through evolution (theistic evolutionists) believe God meant His day was millions of earth's rotations.

Now that we understand more about the nature of time from "Mystery 9," it is clear neither assumption can be correct. In fact, a day (one rotation of the earth) now is not like the day referenced in the book of Numbers; the earth's rotation is slower. One rotation now takes longer than it did in the book of Numbers.

When God created everything, there is no mention of speed or of gravity. So there is no way to relate God's *day* to the days we experience now. But even more interesting, God is describing to us a measure of time that is relative to Him. Since His time may be nothing like time relative to us now, there is no way to conclude that He performed His creative acts in a simple rotation of earth now or if it took Him millions of rotations.

We live and even represent our lives by tracking days; we date nearly everything. God had the ability to create all things at once and did not really require six rotations of the planet to complete it. So the question becomes this: Why would God tell us what He made on His six days, and does it really matter?

His description is not an analogy or allegory. It is not even a metaphor. It is a *construct*, a frame with which we are able to picture how He created everything. It is a wonderful word portrait we can visualize to partially understand the complexity of how He fabricated the world we live in. Beyond that, it is of no consequence.

MYSTERY 11

Heaven

Heaven is a real place. It did not always exist. God, however, always did.

"And He Himself existed before all things, and in Him all things consist (cohere, are held together)" (Colossians 1:17).

At some point in God's time, He decided to create heaven. Once created, He chose to live there. God further created all its inhabitants; living beings who are referred to as *angels*.

There is no reference to angels creating other angels as humans create other humans through procreation. There are no angels with female names in the Bible; angels were neither male nor female.

In fact, when Jesus was explaining the fine points of the resurrection to the Sadducees, He pointed out people are not married or given in marriage in the resurrection; they would be like angels and become the Sons of God:

> *But those who are considered worthy to gain that other world and that future age and to attain to the resurrection from the dead neither marry nor are given in marriage;*
> *For they cannot die again, but they are angel-like and equal to angels. And being sons of and sharers in the resurrection, they are sons of God. (Luke 20:35–36)*

Since sexual relations are only allowed in marriage and there is no marriage in heaven, then those resurrected people do not have sex and do not need to have sexual organs.

The implications are angels need no sexual activity either and never die; consequently, the number created is the exact number there will always be, and there were many.

"But rather, you have come to Mount Zion, even to the city of the living God, the heavenly Jerusalem, and to countless multitudes of angels in festal gathering" (Hebrews 12:22).

Heaven and angels were in existence before God created our current earth and universe. They witnessed God's creative acts.

"Who determined the measures of the earth, if you know? Or who stretched the measuring line upon it?

Upon what were the foundations of it fastened, or who laid its cornerstone,

When the morning stars sang together and all the sons of God shouted for joy?" (Job 38:5–7).

Angels have a definite hierarchy; there are very important ones, less important ones, and average ones. Lucifer (Satan) had the most splendor. However, he chose to be a god and replace the true God (Ezekiel 28:12–18).

His choice demonstrated angels have some degree of free will. In fact, he convinced a third of the angels (who became demons) in heaven to follow him. The result of their rebellion, however, is they all will be expelled from heaven to earth three and a half years into the tribulation period:

> *His tail swept [across the sky] and dragged down a third of the stars and flung them to the earth. And the dragon stationed himself in front of the woman who was about to be delivered, so that he might devour her child as soon as she brought it forth. (Revelation 12:4)*

> *And the huge dragon was cast down and out—that age-old serpent, who is called the Devil*

and Satan, he who is the seducer (deceiver) of all humanity the world over; he was forced out and down to the earth, and his angels were flung out along with him. (Revelation 12:9)

Angels are not all-knowing, nor are they all-powerful. God actually uses the church (the body of believers) to teach them about His wisdom and justice.

"[The purpose is] that through the church the complicated, many-sided wisdom of God in all its infinite variety and innumerable aspects might now be made known to the angelic rulers and authorities (principalities and powers) in the heavenly sphere" (Ephesians 3:10).

Even though heaven is the habitat for angels and will be for eternity, it also contains a temporary place for Christians to reside when they die:

> *In My Father's house there are many dwelling places (homes). If it were not so, I would have told you; for I am going away to prepare a place for you.*
> *And when (if) I go and make ready a place for you, I will come back again and will take you to Myself, that where I am you may be also. (John 14:2–3)*

Now having gained insight into what heaven is, very little understanding of *time* there is provided. People could see each other, so visible light must be there. It may, however, not be like the light we experience today for the source is not stated. There is no mention of night, so angels must not need to sleep.

There are a few things that can be understood about time in heaven. It is eternal. There are two clues to this. First, an angel comes from heaven and shows the Apostle John the new Jerusalem, which is descending from heaven to the eternal, *new earth.*

"Then one of the seven angels who had the seven bowls filled with the seven final plagues (afflictions, calamities) came and spoke to me.

He said, Come with me! I will show you the bride, the Lamb's wife"
(Revelation 21:9).

The second clue is that the saints of God will judge the angels during eternity.

"Do you not know also that we [Christians] are to judge the [very] angels and pronounce opinion between right and wrong [for them]? How much more then [as to] matters pertaining to this world and of this life only!" (1 Corinthians 6:3).

If heaven is eternal, time in heaven must be eternal. But there appears to be a correspondence between time on earth after sin and time in heaven. This is demonstrated by angel visits to earth for special purposes.

Examples are when the angels visited Abraham before destroying Sodom and Gomorrah, when an angel visited Abram and Sarai, when one came to Mary, and when one showed up at the tomb after the resurrection.

But probably the most direct evidence of some correlation is Satan being expelled from heaven three and a half years in the middle of the tribulation (Revelation 12:9) and when an angel was sent to interpret Daniel's vision but was delayed by Satan for twenty-one earth days:

> *Then he said to me, Fear not, Daniel, for from the first day that you set your mind and heart to understand and to humble yourself before your God, your words were heard, and I have come as a consequence of [and in response to] your words.*
>
> *But the prince of the kingdom of Persia withstood me for twenty-one days. Then Michael, one of the chief [of the celestial] princes, came to help me, for I remained there with the kings of Persia. (Daniel 10:12–13)*

This points out that angels actively use their *time.* They are messengers. They defend children, announce things, fight demons, provide protection, and put God-created souls into babies. More about this will be discussed in "Mystery 17."

MYSTERY 12

Hades

As stated earlier, there are two deaths and three lives. The soul is eternal. A human body is merely a vehicle for the soul. When that vehicle ceases to exist (dies), the soul must go somewhere.

After Jesus was resurrected, there was a way for a soul to go directly to heaven: believe on Him and have a spirit born. Then the soul with its spirit proceeds immediately to heaven when the body dies.

But before Jesus, and for all those who have not been given a chance to know Jesus, God created a temporary place for souls to reside—Hades.

There are two parts of Hades: torments and paradise. Paul points this out in his letter to the Corinthians; *paradise* is the third heaven (2 Corinthians 12:2–4). The following provides detailed information about Hades:

> *The time came when the beggar died and the angels carried him to Abraham's side. The rich man also died and was buried. In Hades, where he was in torment, he looked up and saw Abraham far away, with Lazarus by his side. So he called to him, 'Father Abraham, have pity on me and send Lazarus to dip the tip of his finger in water and cool my tongue, because I am in agony in this fire.'*

"But Abraham replied, 'Son, remember that in your lifetime you received your good things, while Lazarus received bad things, but now he is comforted here and you are in agony. And besides all this, between us and you a great chasm has been set in place, so that those who want to go from here to you cannot, nor can anyone cross over from there to us.' (Luke 16:22–26 NIV)

Summarizing the provided information, people from both parts can see one another, talk to each other, but cannot visit from one side to the other because they are separated by a large void.

Souls have a projected image and are recognizable. People from different times of death can mingle together with those of other times. Souls can physically touch each other and can remember their life on earth. People in torments are in pain and agony.

Hades is first referenced in Genesis 37:35.

"And all his sons and daughters attempted to console him, but he refused to be comforted and said, I will go down to Sheol (the place of the dead) to my son mourning. And his father wept for him."

God places people in Hades, either in torments or in paradise, in whatever way He wants. The Scriptures do not tell us how God makes such a decision, but it is likely based upon their faith as demonstrated by what they did during their lifetimes.

However, the souls of aborted babies, of babies who die in childbirth, of children who die or are killed at a young age, of some people who never become intellectually more than a child because of special needs, or of those who never had an opportunity to hear the Gospel are placed into paradise.

They will be given maturity, so they are intellectually able to understand the Gospel. The reason for this is a just God must give them a chance to believe on Jesus and enter heaven:

Will You show wonders to the dead? Shall the departed arise and praise You? Selah [pause, and calmly think of that]!

Shall Your steadfast love be declared in the grave? Or Your faithfulness in Abaddon (Sheol, as a place of ruin and destruction)? (Psalm 88:10–11)

The narrowness of salvation is presented in John 14:6.

"Jesus said to him, I am the Way and the Truth and the Life; no one comes to the Father except by (through) Me."

And the uniqueness of Jesus is described in Acts 4:12.

"For there is no other name under heaven given among men by and in which we must be saved."

In order for all souls to hear the Gospel, Jesus went to paradise when His body died.

"Then he said, 'Jesus, remember me when you come into your kingdom.' Jesus answered him, 'Truly I tell you, today you will be with me in paradise'" (Luke 23:42–43).

After Jesus died on the cross and went there, He spent three days preaching to those souls who had been collected together. He presented all He had done for their salvation and gave them a chance to accept it.

There were two specific groups to whom Jesus spoke. One set were those souls who were placed in Hades before the great flood—all the dead starting with Abel to all those who drowned in the flood.

"In which He went and preached to the spirits in prison, [The souls of those] who long before in the days of Noah had been disobedient, when God's patience waited during the building of the ark in which a few [people], actually eight in number, were saved through water" (1 Peter 3:19–20).

A second set of those in paradise receiving the Gospel was everyone from Noah to the last person to be placed there who never had fortuity to hear it. They were given a chance and could decide for Christ.

"But they will have to give account to him who is ready to judge the living and the dead. For this is the reason the gospel was preached even to those who are now dead, so that they might be judged according to human standards in regard to the body, but live according to God in regard to the spirit" (1 Peter 4:5–6 NIV).

Since all those souls could accept Christ's sacrifice, those who believed were rewarded, given spirits, and could legitimately be brought into heaven through Jesus's name:

> *But to each one of us grace has been given as Christ apportioned it. This is why it says: 'When he ascended on high, he took many captives and gave gifts to his people.' (What does 'he ascended' mean except that he also descended to the lower, earthly regions? He who descended is the very one who ascended higher than all the heavens, in order to fill the whole universe.) (Ephesians 4:7–10 NIV)*

Through all of our recorded time after sin entered the world, Hades existed and still exists to collect the souls of people who did not have a chance to hear the Gospel.

Unfortunately, it also has an area (*torments*) to hold those souls who heard the Gospel and did not choose to accept Christ's sacrifice before dying. They will remain there until the final judgment, just before death and Hades are placed into the lake of fire (Revelation 20:14).

Time in Hades is not the same as our current time and must be much shorter than what we experience now. Granted, it started with Abel's death and ends just before God creates a new heaven and earth.

However, time is different because all souls (those living before Jesus was crucified and all those after) can commingle together. The one and only time Jesus went to paradise, they all came together to hear His message of salvation.

MYSTERY 13

The Preflood World

The preflood world is described in Genesis 1–6. Those chapters are crammed with strange information, but the details are quite sparse. So sparse it is difficult to completely unpack what is being described. In a nutshell, Adam and Eve were created, then sinned, which changed everything. The best way to start unraveling the mystery of the preflood world is to start with Cain.

The conventional view is Cain was born of Adam and Eve and began the population growth of the preflood world. Adam and Eve had a few baby girls, then Cain was born, followed by Abel. After they had grown up, Cain killed Abel. God punished Cain, sentencing him to wander in the land of Nod. Cain married his sister.

So the mystery begins with God's punishment for Cain killing Abel.

"When you till the ground, it shall no longer yield to you its strength; you shall be a fugitive and a vagabond on the earth [in perpetual exile, a degraded outcast]" (Genesis 4:12).

Of course, Cain complained.

"Then Cain said to the Lord, My punishment is greater than I can bear.

Behold, You have driven me out this day from the face of the land, and from Your face I will be hidden; and I will be a fugitive and a vagabond and a wanderer on the earth, and whoever finds me will kill me" (Genesis 4:13–14).

Then God modified the sentence.

"And the Lord said to him, Therefore, if anyone kills Cain, vengeance shall be taken on him sevenfold. And the Lord set a mark or sign upon Cain, lest anyone finding him should kill him. So Cain went away from the presence of the Lord and dwelt in the land of Nod [wandering], east of Eden" (Genesis 4:15–16).

The first problem encountered here is who was Cain afraid might find him and kill him? He is supposed to be the first man of the preflood world and is not even married yet. There would not be anyone on earth to *find* him and kill him for countless years.

The second problem is Cain is supposed to be a *restless wanderer*. But what does he really do?

"And Cain's wife [one of Adam's offspring] became pregnant and bore Enoch; and Cain built a city and named it after his son Enoch" (Genesis 4:17).

Cain was not wandering but building a city. People who live in cities do not wander. Even more puzzling, it is a *city*, not a village or a town, but a city.

Cities have a large number of citizens, many dwellings, infrastructures, roads, waste removal, government, and commerce. Who does Cain think will live in his city? If he must wait many years for the preflood society to become large enough, why bother?

The third problem is what type of Adam's offspring is Cain's wife. She cannot be his sister.

"You shall not have intercourse with or uncover the nakedness of your sister, the daughter of your father or of your mother, whether born at home or born abroad" (Leviticus 18:9).

The explanation must be there existed a *pre-sin* society.

MYSTERY 19

The Pre-Sin Society

In order to examine how a pre-sin society came about, one must understand who the *Sons of God* are in Genesis 6.

"The sons of God saw that the daughters of men were fair, and they took wives of all they desired and chose" (Genesis 6:2).

The normal technique of trying to understand who they could be is to find other places in the Bible where *Sons of God* are mentioned. The problem is, there are so many different places with totally different meanings it is impossible to apply any one of them to explain Genesis 6.

"For [even the whole] creation (all nature) waits expectantly and longs earnestly for God's sons to be made known [waits for the revealing, the disclosing of their sonship]" (Romans 8:19).

Here, the Apostle Paul is describing those believers in Jesus who will be collected together, and a new age will begin where there is no longer death due to aging.

"I said, You are gods [since you judge on My behalf, as My representatives]; indeed, all of you are children of the Most High" (Psalm 82:6).

This refers to earthly judges who God has appointed but act as if they are gods by ignoring the laws of the nation and imposing their own will.

"He answered, Behold, I see four men loose, walking in the midst of the fire, and they are not hurt! And the form of the fourth is like a son of the gods!" (Daniel 3:25).

Here, Nebuchadnezzar describes a person who is saving Shadrach, Meshach, and Abednego from a fiery furnace.

"When the morning stars sang together and all the sons of God shouted for joy?" (Job 38:7).

Here they appear to be angels.

"Yet the number of the children of Israel shall be as the sand of the sea, which cannot be measured or numbered; and instead of it being said to them, You are not My people, it shall be said to them, Sons of the Living God!" (Hosea 1:10).

Here, it is the prediction that God's judgment on Israel and Judah (being scattered among the nations) will end, and they will again be gathered together and be labeled as sons.

"For God so greatly loved and dearly prized the world that He [even] gave up His only begotten (unique) Son, so that whoever believes in (trusts in, clings to, relies on) Him shall not perish (come to destruction, be lost) but have eternal (everlasting) life" (John 3:16).

Here it is—Jesus, God Himself in human form.

"For they cannot die again, but they are angel-like and equal to angels. And being sons of and sharers in the resurrection, they are sons of God" (Luke 20:36).

Here, Jesus is describing resurrected humans in heaven.

It is clear the *sons* in Genesis 6 cannot be angels (who have no sex organs), Jesus, Israel, resurrected humans, a personal savior, gathered believers, or earthly judges. Since examining other uses of the label *Sons of God* does not help, there must be a different explanation; one that fits the rest of what is described in Genesis 6.

This can be determined in the normal, inductive manner; collect the facts, then draw the most probable conclusion that encompasses all those facts:

1. Nothing aged or died from old age before the first sin (Romans 8:19–22).
2. If nothing aged, then Adam and Eve could have lived for many years (maybe even thousands or millions of years) before the first sin.

3. Genesis 3:20 states that Eve was given her name because she was the mother of all living. (Note: The Bible does not state that Adam was the father of all living.)
4. Eve was already having babies before the first sin (Genesis 3:16).
5. Her babies formed with Adam were all girls because Cain was the first boy they produced together (Genesis 4:1).
6. Half brothers and half sisters could marry and reproduce; acceptable to God for Abram and Sarai were half brother and half sister (Genesis 20:12).
7. The Holy Spirit impregnated Mary.

"Then the angel said to her, The Holy Spirit will come upon you, and the power of the Most High will overshadow you [like a shining cloud]; and so the holy (pure, sinless) Thing (Offspring) which shall be born of you will be called the Son of God" (Luke 1:35).

The conclusion is God must have impregnated Eve at least twice (*Sons*) and probably numerous times in the possible thousands or millions of years before the first sin. Those *Sons* mated with Adam and Eve's girls (half sisters) and had children, who also had children, until a large number of people existed—a pre-sin society.

Those people could see Cain's God-placed sign and be prevented from killing him. Some could live in Cain's city. And Cain's wife was a distant relative born from many iterations of births and marriages, rather than his sister.

This concept is criticized by some from the evangelical community as a degradation of the birth of Jesus. Most believe that when the Apostle John says Jesus is the Son of God, there are no other sons. But the list above clearly shows there are others referenced.

Remember from "Mystery 1," their belief is not what John 3:16 states.

It states that "He gave up His only-begotten (unique) Son, so that whoever believes…" Jesus clearly is being described as God's unique son. The Greek word translated *only begotten* is *monogenes* and means *uniquely born*. It does not mean *uniquely conceived*.

Jesus's uniqueness is He was the only person conceived in a virgin who had the sin principle but was born sinless, not taking on that virgin's fallen nature (no living spirit). He was the only *Son* designated to be able to *pay* for the trespasses of all humanity. There was none before Him, nor will there be any after Him.

Also remember, technically speaking, Jesus is not God's *Son*, but God Himself.

Therefore, God could have conceived other sons. Eve was not a virgin, and her spirit had not yet died. So the Holy Spirit impregnating her and producing *Sons of God* would in no way impact the miracle of Jesus's birth and His ability to be the only one qualified to die to pay for mankind's sins.

Time during the pre-sin society would be quite different. Since there was no aging, biology and physics would be different. Hence, time would be different:

> *For [even the whole] creation (all nature) waits expectantly and longs earnestly for God's sons to be made known [waits for the revealing, the disclosing of their sonship].*
>
> *For the creation (nature) was subjected to frailty (to futility, condemned to frustration), not because of some intentional fault on its part, but by the will of Him Who so subjected it—[yet] with the hope*
>
> *That nature (creation) itself will be set free from its bondage to decay and corruption [and gain an entrance] into the glorious freedom of God's children.*
>
> *We know that the whole creation [of irrational creatures] has been moaning together in the pains of labor until now. (Romans 8:19–22)*

The stunning and silly extension of not understanding the historical lack of *age* comes about when scientists attempt to date the *age* of fossils, or for that matter, the earth itself.

The most common atomic dating methods currently use a ratio of one radioactive isotope relative to a certain other one. The ratios are assumed to be *set* in a specific way at the *time* the item was created and when it died (but nothing died due to old age). This is a big assumption since God may have created things with any ratio of isotopes He wanted.

The methods then measure that particular ratio in today's definition of *days* and extrapolate backward the number of today's *days* to determine how *old* the item was when it died. Clearly, since historical *days* are not like today's *days,* the extrapolation cannot be accurate.

But an even more important consideration is that because *time* was different before the first sin, physics was likely different also. Radioactive decay (if there even was any then) would also be different.

About the only information available to reckon some details about pre-sin *time* is that the earth was spinning faster than what we are currently experiencing. This would result in days being shorter, thus people's *ages* appear longer than what they would be measured today on a slower spinning globe.

Another thing would be if planet movement was the same then as we observe now; earth could not be very old, for the moon is slowly moving away from the earth. Assuming the rate of movement was the same then, it can be calculated (backward) to the time when the moon was very close to earth about twelve thousand years ago. The planet then could not be older than that calculation.

But God could have periodically reset His creation to *factory settings*. That is, He could have occasionally restarted all planetary movements as they were when He had originally created them. The conclusion is that before the first sin was committed, time, its nature, and its effects are basically unknown and could not be exactly as the time we now experience.

MYSTERY 15

The Preflood Society

Cain was the beginning of the *post-sin, preflood* society. As his children had children (and so on), a population of individuals grew to be quite large. The result was the pre-sin society began to mingle with the post-sin one.

"When human beings began to increase in number on the earth and daughters were born to them, the sons of God saw that the daughters of humans were beautiful, and they married any of them they chose" (Genesis 6:1–2 NIV).

The pre-sin group still had spirits that were alive. And even though creation began to age and move toward death, those people did not. This would explain the odd passage about death.

"Then the LORD said, 'My Spirit will not contend with humans forever, for they are mortal; their days will be a hundred and twenty years'" (Genesis 6:3 NIV).

This statement causes confusion because in the genealogy of Adam (Genesis 5), all those listed lived much longer than 120 years. Another perplexing thing about this statement is the Holy Spirit must be struggling with a set of people then in a different way than He dealt with the rest of preflood (and for that matter post-flood) people.

The pre-sin society still had a spirit, and the Holy Spirit was still connected to it. That connection would result in a different dynamic between those people and God versus post-sin ones.

Add to that, those pre-sin people did not get old and die. Then God's death sentence on them makes sense. They were still just humans (albeit special), so God declares they might not get old and die, but He would only allow them to stay alive 120 years.

Of course, these people would go directly into heaven at death for their souls were infinite and they had not sinned, so their spirits were alive. They would be like angels.

"Now there was a day when the sons (the angels) of God came to present themselves before the Lord, and Satan (the adversary and accuser) also came among them" (Job 1:6).

This limit on their mortal lives assured the preflood society would eventually consist of only post-sin humans but presented a problem with the children of pre-sin and post-sin individuals.

"The Nephilim were on the earth in those days—and also after- ward—when the sons of God went to the daughters of humans and had children by them. They were the heroes of old, men of renown" (Genesis 6:4 NIV).

The Sons of God had spirits, but the daughters of men did not. The difficulty comes about when those two types mate. Do their children have spirits or not? The answer comes from understand- ing the definition of *Nephilim*. The Hebrew Bible translates it as *the fallen ones.*

Therefore, the children of the Sons of God and daughters of men with no spirit are all *fallen* (i.e., have no spirits). They are special because of their father's uniqueness and become famous for a host of reasons—men of renown. But they have no spirits.

By examining the genealogies from Adam to Noah, the post- sin, preflood society spanned between 1,500 and 2,000 years. The Bible presents very little information about those people other than they became quite sinful. So much so God decided to eliminate all of them except Noah and his family.

It is interesting and perhaps informative to think a little about what such a society was like:

1. There were no fossil fuels. As of this writing, the US has about six thousand items in general use made from oil. That society would have none of them.
2. The earth had no seasons; hence, fruits and vegetables were available year-round.
3. Animal instincts would be unrestrained, and some would eat others. Humans would kill and eat animals.
4. There was only one language.
5. There was no rain, and the sun would be somewhat blocked by the mist rising from the ground. This would block UV rays from the sun, allowing people to live much longer than now.
6. The temperature would be like tropical islands are today.
7. There would be no storms.
8. Lush and giant vegetation covered the earth, raising oxygen levels.
9. People and animals could grow very large because of reduced UV rays and increased oxygen.

Using typical birth rates currently known, there were likely a billion people born before the flood. Since they lived longer than we do now, the number was probably much higher.

For a point of reference, about five to seven hundred years passed after the flood before construction of the Tower of Babel began. God's response was interesting:

> *And the Lord said, Behold, they are one people and they have all one language; and this is only the beginning of what they will do, and now nothing they have imagined they can do will be impossible for them. Come, let Us go down and there confound (mix up, confuse) their language, that they may not understand one another's speech. (Genesis 11:6–7)*

God did not say human speech needed to be confounded *again*, proving the preflood society had only one language. But with one language, God stated humans could accomplish whatever they imagined.

If it took the post-flood society five hundred years to develop the technology to build the tower, imagine what the preflood peoples could do in 1,500 to 2,000 years with a single language. Think about the scientific advancements the United States has accomplished in the last two hundred years.

But even more incredible, some of the children of the Sons of God (men of renown) had to be famous for their scientific prowess. Starting the development of science and technology with people much smarter than Einstein and building on that knowledge (with a single language) for two thousand years would yield incredible advancements.

Jesus's statement about the end-times assures they achieved space travel.

"And He will send out His angels with a loud trumpet call, and they will gather His elect (His chosen ones) from the four winds, [even] from one end of the universe to the other" (Matthew 24:31).

It could also explain multiple sightings of unidentified flying objects (UFOs) reported by our military which exhibit technology far superior to ours. Based on the recent government-released videos, they obviously have harnessed (controlled) gravity and eliminated the effects of friction, allowing great speed, incredible maneuverability, and the ability to pass through any medium with ease.

Remember, Eve was stated to be the mother of all living humans (Genesis 3:20). UFOs are created and navigated by living beings. Therefore, their mother could have been Eve. Some preflood beings must have moved before the flood to other galaxies to live and perhaps are simply occasionally visiting their world of origin.

The problem with this explanation, however, is those people have not contacted us. Another problem is there is no record of seeing UFOs coming from outer space to earth.

As stated, Eve was the mother of all living after God created Adam and Eve. But angels are alive and were created by God before our heaven and earth. Therefore, an alternate explanation of UFOs is they are craft created and piloted by demons.

Obviously, they would not need such vehicles because there is ample evidence in the Bible they can just *appear* on earth at will. Also, angels are not subject to the laws of physics. But Satan could be "programming" humankind to believe a tremendous lie revealed during the tribulation period.

For some reason, artists have repeatedly pictured aliens from another planet as being small, bald, green, not having ears, having two slits replacing a nose, having protruding eyes, and having a large mouth, looking much like the head of a frog:

> *And I saw three loathsome spirits like frogs, [leaping] from the mouth of the dragon and from the mouth of the beast and from the mouth of the false prophet.*
>
> *For really they are the spirits of demons that perform signs (wonders, miracles). And they go forth to the rulers and leaders all over the world, to gather them together for war on the great day of God the Almighty. (Revelation 16:13–14)*

It could be during the end-times, Satan (through the words of the antichrist and the false prophet) introduces aliens from *another planet* who are far superior to mankind (can do wonders). Those apparent *extraterrestrials* might even lessen the impact of the Rapture by explaining they had removed some people from earth to "purify" humanity.

Their knowledge and abilities cloud people's reasoning, so they can push Satan's deceitful agenda of a great final conflict. They instruct mankind on whom they should war against. The enemy appears to be the armies of the East, but they always intended to turn it into a conflict with God.

"Then I saw the beast and the rulers and leaders of the earth with their troops mustered to go into battle and make war against Him Who is mounted on the horse and against His troops" (Revelation 19:19).

Remember, Jess warned about this.

"For false Christs and false prophets will arise, and they will show great signs and wonders so as to deceive and lead astray, if possible, even the elect (God's chosen ones)" (Matthew 24:24).

Returning to the preflood society's technological abilities, skeptics would challenge their abilities by saying if they were so advanced, there would be evidence of it somewhere on the planet. That evidence would be required to have survived the *great flood*. A quick Google search for *unexplained ancient mysteries* produced the following examples:

1. About a hundred metal spheres were found in South Africa. Their exterior was so hard (metal hardness) that a steel point could not etch it, but the interior was soft. They were found in a geological layer thought to be 2.8 billion years old.

2. A zinc-silver vessel was found in solid rock in Massachusetts. The rock was judged to be five hundred million years old.

3. A mechanism found near the Antikythera Island is an incredible machine of finely calibrated gears thought to be more than two thousand years old. It is an ancient computer that can calculate a wealth of astronomical information.

4. A wedge was found near the town of Aiud in Romania, more than thirty-three feet underground and in direct association with mastodon fossils. The wedge is unique in that it's almost 90 percent metallic aluminum (which people now only began producing around two hundred years ago) but coated in four-hundred-year-old aluminum oxide and found with bones of an animal that went extinct at least eleven thousand years ago.

5. A giant circular structure thirty feet underwater was found in the Sea of Galilee. The basaltic structure appears to have been built on the land with many large stones then sub-

merged, and it could be between two thousand and twelve thousand years old.

6. A collection of jars from at least 250 BC found in Iraq has the outer clay jar stoppered with asphalt but contained an iron rod placed inside a copper tube. When the jar is filled with vinegar, it can hold a charge—like a battery.

7. A sprawling underwater city was found submerged just off the coast of Yonaguni Jima, Japan. It is believed to be more than five thousand years old. It has everything from a large stone gateway to carved stairways and streets to vaulting towers.

8. A series of massive drawings etched into rocks on the earth, numbering into the thousands, can still be observed (especially from the air) in Western Bolivia. The lines, between three to ten feet wide individually, connect about 8,700 square miles via an intricate weblike design.

9. Mysterious stone spheres can still be found in the Diquis Delta of Costa Rica. These objects range in size from a few centimeters to over two meters in diameter with some weighing as much as sixteen tons. All of the spheres are man-made objects formed from the igneous stone known as granodiorite.

10. Outside of Cuzco, Peru, there is a remarkable walled fortress constructed out of perfectly fitted boulders, some weighing over two hundred tons. Known as Saksaywayman, the exact construction date is unknown, although the structure is ancient enough to predate the Incas themselves. The gaps between the rocks are so thin that a piece of paper will not even fit between them.

11. A structure was discovered in Turkey which is thought to be a temple made from massive carved stones dating back to 11,000 BC. It predates Stonehenge by six thousand years. The temple was built before the advent of metal tools or even pottery.

12. Extensive underground networks and even entire cities have been found all over the world.
    a) Derinkuyu in Cappadocia, Turkey is probably the largest underground city that has been discovered to date. It spans more than eight levels going as deep as eighty meters with more than six hundred entrances to the surface.
    b) In Egypt, the Giza Plateau has an enormous underground system that is a combination of man-made caverns and tunnels as well as subterranean rivers and passages.
    c) In Guatemala, eight hundred kilometers worth of tunnels have been mapped underneath the Mayan pyramid complex at Tikal.
    d) Twenty-four man-made caves were discovered in China, displaying incredible craftsmanship that would have involved the excavation of thirty-six thousand cubic meters of stone.
    e) Archaeologists have uncovered thousands of Stone Age underground tunnels, stretching across Europe.
13. In Puma Punku, Bolivia, enormous blocks weighing up to eight hundred tons were found. They have perfectly straight edges that lock precisely into each other and contain no chisel marks. They are estimated to be seventeen thousand years old.
14. Razor-sharp crystal rock daggers and arrowheads were found near Seville, Spain thought to be five thousand years old.

This is ample evidence the preflood society was far more advanced than ours today.

MYSTERY 16

The Great Flood

The preflood society became so sinful and corrupt, God decided to eliminate them and start over with eight righteous people: Noah and his wife plus his three sons and their wives:

> *So the Lord said, I will destroy, blot out, and wipe away mankind, whom I have created from the face of the ground—not only man, [but] the beasts and the creeping things and the birds of the air—for it grieves Me and makes Me regretful that I have made them.*
>
> *But Noah found grace (favor) in the eyes of the Lord. (Genesis 6:7–8)*

This incredible act of annihilating the entire population of the earth is of immense importance. The great tribulation period described in the book of Revelation is shockingly harsh, violent, and devastating.

Many people will die or be killed. However, even during the tribulation, a smaller percentage of mankind will be exterminated than those in the great flood because the end-time devastation is limited.

"And if those days had not been shortened, no human being would endure and survive, but for the sake of the elect [God's chosen ones] those days will be shortened" (Matthew 24:22).

The intent of the flood was to destroy all of mankind and land animals on earth except for those whom God had selected. They were placed inside an ark, a large boat, which He specifically designed, and Noah built.

Although this remarkable event of an earth-wide flood is so crucial to understanding the Bible, many people believe it is a made-up story that did not happen and could never happen. The naysayers provide skepticism and unbelief.

Occasionally, some attempt to apply logic to prove a great flood could never happen, such as calculating how many inches of rain per hour would have to fall in forty days and forty nights to generate enough water to cover Mount Everest, the highest mountain on earth (of course assuming it existed before the flood).

Making a few credible assumptions on volume and using a reasonable mathematical equation, they calculate that it would require fourteen trillion inches of rain an hour to cover the earth's surface to a height equal to Mount Everest in the limited time allowed.

"[In fact] the waters became fifteen cubits higher, as the high hills were covered" (Genesis 7:20).

And of course, to underscore how ridiculous this sounds, doubters question how it could rain that much, where it all came from, and where all that water went in the five months Noah was in the ark before seeing land.

Many skeptics are unbelievers or ones who only have a kindergartener's understanding of the Bible. But in this case, they miss a key element of logic. If one starts with an incorrect premise (rain caused the flood), the conclusion is never true.

"In the year 600 of Noah's life, in the seventeenth day of the second month, that same day all the fountains of the great deep were broken up and burst forth, and the windows and floodgates of the heavens were opened" (Genesis 7:11).

This verse describes the occurrence of a cataclysmic event. There is no mention of rain. What is being described is a disaster involving the earth's great deep—a violent collision of the earth's water and land. Then it rained forty days and nights afterward.

"And it rained upon the earth forty days and forty nights" (Genesis 7:12).

The flood was already occurring, and whatever triggered it generated the falling of rain for all those days and nights, the amount inconsequential.

The catastrophic event that caused the flood is easy to understand. Consider a miniature globe of the planet earth. It is always shown tilted, about twenty-four degrees off perpendicular. That tilt is what causes the seasons.

When God created the earth, He created it with no tilt. In executing judgment upon the perverse and wicked people alive at that time, He chose to instantly tilt the earth.

To get a good visual sense of this, fix an object to the inside bottom of a bowl so it is stationary. Fill the bowl with water to just below the top of the fixed object. Place a slip of paper on the water away from the object as a reference point. Tip the bowl to one side quickly.

The result demonstrates what happened when God caused the earth to tilt twenty-four degrees off perpendicular. The fixed object, representing the land, slips into the water, but the reference piece of paper, representing earth's water, barely moves. The water did not instantly move with the landmasses because it was not attached.

The *great deep* described in the Bible is the ocean's reservoirs which appear to burst forth when the land is forcibly thrust into them.

There certainly is enough water in them to cover Mount Everest. The deepest known point in the earth's oceans is called the Mariana Trench. It is over thirty-six thousand feet deep. If one could put Mount Everest into that trench, it would be totally covered by more than one mile of water.

The skeptic is proven utterly wrong. There is no need to worry about how it could rain fourteen trillion inches an hour or where the rain came from because the flood was not caused by rain.

Earth (land) was forced into the oceans when God tilted it. And of course, after the tilt, the oceans gradually flowed back to positions among the newly formed land structures; hence, there is no concern for where all the flood water went.

When God created the earth, not only was there no tilt but there was only one continent.

"God called the dry land Earth, and the accumulated waters He called Seas. And God saw that this was good (fitting, admirable) and He approved it" (Genesis 1:10).

However, the tilting of the earth would have been more than cataclysmic. It would have been devastating. Earth's tectonic plates shifted and relocated. Volcanoes erupted. Hydrothermal vents in the sea opened.

The single continent split and broke apart into several smaller ones. Various islands were formed. Mountains and deep valleys were created. In short, the basic geography of the earth now would have been the result of this disastrous event.

MYSTERY 17

Eternity

Continuing from "Mystery 7," at the end of the thousand-year period, Jesus and all believers will return to heaven, and Satan will be released from his prison.

"And when the thousand years are completed, Satan will be released from his place of confinement" (Revelation 20:7).

The center of religion will be located in the rebuilt city of Jerusalem. Satan will again deceive many of the people of earth.

The generation of those who had lived under the saint's judging and Jesus's ruling will die, giving way for Satan to once again convince people the inhabitants of Jerusalem are evil and must be destroyed.

That will take longer than the forty years the Israelites wandered in the desert until the generation refusing to enter the promised land died, for people will be living much longer then.

"There shall no more be in it an infant who lives but a few days, or an old man who dies prematurely; for the child shall die a hundred years old, and the sinner who dies when only a hundred years old shall be [thought only a child, cut off because he is] accursed" (Isaiah 65:20).

But after hundreds of years, Satan will cause a worldwide rebellion; eventually, he incites the deceived people to war against Jerusalem to destroy it and those in it:

> *And he will go forth to deceive and seduce and*
> *lead astray the nations which are in the four quar-*

> *ters of the earth—Gog and Magog—to muster them*
> *for war; their number is like the sand of the sea.*
>
> *And they swarmed up over the broad plain*
> *of the earth and encircled the fortress (camp) of*
> *God's people (the saints) and the beloved city; but*
> *fire descended from heaven and consumed them.*
> *(Revelation 20:8–9)*

God will intervene and end the onslaught of humanity with fire from heaven. The fire will consume all the multitudes gathered together to capture and destroy Jerusalem.

It will not destroy the inhabitants of Jerusalem. It also will not destroy babies and children, old people too feeble to join the nation's armies, women who cared for children, and others who did not believe Satan's lies.

When that fire comes down from heaven, the material universe as we know it will end. Most likely God will simply stop holding together the atoms He used to create our world. There will be an astonishing *nuclear* explosion.

"But the day of the Lord will come like a thief, and then the heavens will vanish (pass away) with a thunderous crash, and the [material] elements [of the universe] will be dissolved with fire, and the earth and the works that are upon it will be burned up" (2 Peter 3:10).

However, God's chosen ones will be transferred to a *new earth* located in a *new heaven* (universe). Although all will be located on the *new earth*, they will live in two separate places. The saints with glorified bodies will live in the new Jerusalem with God living among them:

> *Then I saw a new sky (heaven) and a new*
> *earth, for the former sky and the former earth had*
> *passed away (vanished), and there no longer existed*
> *any sea.*
>
> *And I saw the holy city, the new Jerusalem,*
> *descending out of heaven from God, all arrayed like*
> *a bride beautified and adorned for her husband;*

> *Then I heard a mighty voice from the throne*
> *and I perceived its distinct words, saying, See!*
> *The abode of God is with men, and He will live*
> *(encamp, tent) among them; and they shall be His*
> *people, and God shall personally be with them and*
> *be their God. (Revelation 21:1–3)*

All the people who were alive in Jerusalem under attack by the deceived populations, along with all the people who were not deceived by Satan (those judged worthy), will be placed on the *new earth* outside of the new Jerusalem with mature spirits.

There they will live as God intended Adam and Eve to exist. There will be no human death and no sin. The people will greatly multiply and form nations with hierarchal leadership that will not have the same language.

This begins eternity. The people of God living in the new Jerusalem will live forever with Him and will reign (not as judges, but as kings) over the nations formed from those surviving the holocaust:

> *There shall no longer exist there anything that*
> *is accursed (detestable, foul, offensive, impure, hate-*
> *ful, or horrible). But the throne of God and of the*
> *Lamb shall be in it, and His servants shall worship*
> *Him [pay divine honors to Him and do Him holy*
> *service].*
> *They shall see His face, and His name shall be*
> *on their foreheads.*
> *And there shall be no more night; they have*
> *no need for lamplight or sunlight, for the Lord God*
> *will illuminate them and be their light, and they*
> *shall reign [as kings] forever and ever (through the*
> *eternities of the eternities). (Revelation 22:3–5)*

People will love each other. There will be no hate, war, or injustice. Everyone will have a purpose and be productive. No one will be depressed. People will grow to maturity physically, emotionally, and spiritually. They will have children, raise them in love, and cherish the family unit. They will create great works of art—paintings, sculpture, etc.

There will be no oceans which will make the climate different (but perfect). However, having no oceans does not mean God will reduce anything else He originally created; God never does less, but always more. The *new* earth will also teem with life as in our beginning; new species will be created as well of those we experience as extinct will again thrive. There will be beautiful flowers, vegetation, trees, and bushes.

Animals will be nurtured, will be used for food, and for pets. They will have whatever instincts God wants and will be controlled by humans. The world will be in perfect balance.

Humans will have the same senses as we do currently but will have added capacities. Sight will include colors from the current visible spectrum plus ones not being able to be seen now. Tasting will be more pronounced. Hearing will be more accurate. Smelling will be enhanced.

People will develop the ability to travel throughout the new universe. They will experience God's glory in a fuller way than we can now. All will come to know God in the way He originally planned.

I challenge you to add to the above list. After imagining how wonderful you think it will be, recall Paul's words:

> *But, on the contrary, as the Scripture says, What eye has not seen and ear has not heard and has not entered into the heart of man, [all that] God has prepared (made and keeps ready) for those who love Him [who hold Him in affectionate reverence, promptly obeying Him and gratefully recognizing the benefits He has bestowed]. (1 Corinthians 2:9)*

In other words, no matter how perfect we can imagine eternity with God, it will be much better. Eternity, in short, will be so incredibly awesome that we will experience God's blessings forever.

The new Jerusalem will be huge.

"The city lies in a square, its length being the same as its width. And he measured the city with his reed—12,000 stadia (about 1,500 miles); its length and width and height are the same" (Revelation 21:16).

The city is about fifteen hundred miles long by fifteen hundred miles wide by fifteen hundred miles high. The shape is likely a cube. If so, there would be enough room for 3.4 billion saints to live in it, each having one cubic mile. To put this in perspective, one square mile contains 640 acres.

For reference, the International Space Station is about 250 miles above the earth. The new Jerusalem will be six times higher. Using distance on an existing US map, the walls would extend from Philadelphia to Denver and from Chicago to Miami.

Worship will be dramatically changed.

"I saw no temple in the city, for the Lord God Omnipotent [Himself] and the Lamb [Himself] are its temple" (Revelation 21:22).

The measure of time in the new earth and the new universe will be different, for there will be no sun or moon.

"And the city has no need of the sun nor of the moon to give light to it, for the splendor and radiance (glory) of God illuminate it, and the Lamb is its lamp" (Revelation 21:23).

Physics and time will be different because of no death and no sun or moon.

The people who will be living outside the city will bring their splendor, glory, and honor into the new Jerusalem at any time for there will be no night:

> *And the city has no need of the sun nor of the moon to give light to it, for the splendor and radiance (glory) of God illuminate it, and the Lamb is its lamp.*
>
> *The nations shall walk by its light and the rulers and leaders of the earth shall bring into it their glory. (Revelation 21:23–24)*

Since there will be no oceans, the nations will have rivers, ponds, and lakes for water. The people outside of the city will have problems of some kind, perhaps accidents, for they will require some type of healing. When needed, the leaves from the *trees of life* along the river of *the water of life* will be used:

> Then he showed me the river whose waters give life, sparkling like crystal, flowing out from the throne of God and of the Lamb
>
> Through the middle of the broadway of the city; also, on either side of the river was the tree of life with its twelve varieties of fruit, yielding each month its fresh crop; and the leaves of the tree were for the healing and the restoration of the nations. *(Revelation 22:1–2).*

Existence in the *new heaven* and *new earth* will be incredible. Do not miss this magnificent opportunity. Believe (i.e., trust in, rely on, and adhere to) Jesus!

ABOUT THE AUTHOR

Larry Massa has authored four previous books, one a best seller. He is a longtime teacher and Christian leader. He has a gift for being able to understand biblical complexities and provide clear interpretations. His blogs on the website crazyaboutgod.com are widely read and facilitate deeper biblical understanding.

Lightning Source UK Ltd.
Milton Keynes UK
UKHW010734070223
416609UK00002B/434